NEW SPAS AND RESORTS

NEW SPAS AND RESORTS

Daniela Santos Quartino

COLLINS|DESIGN
An Imprint of HarperCollins*Publishers*

NEW SPAS AND RESORTS
Copyright © 2007 by COLLINS DESIGN and LOFT Publications

All rights reserved. No part of this book may be used or reproduced in any manner whatsoever,
without written permission except in the case of brief quotations embodied in critical articles and reviews.
For information, address Collins Design, 10 East 53rd Street, New York, NY 10022.

HarperCollins books may be purchased for educational, business, or sales promotional use.
For information, please write: Special Markets Department, HarperCollins Publishers,
10 East 53rd Street, New York, NY 10022.

First edition published in 2007 by:
Loft Publications
Via Laietana 32 4º of. 104
08003 Barcelona, Spain
Tel.: +34 932 688 088
Fax: +34 932 680 425
www.loftpublications.com

English language edition first published in 2007 by:
Collins Design
An Imprint of HarperCollins*Publishers*
10 East 53rd Street
New York, NY 10022
Tel.: (212) 207-7000
Fax: (212) 207-7654
collinsdesign@harpercollins.com
www.harpercollins.com

Distributed throughout the world by:
HarperCollins*Publishers*
10 East 53rd Street
New York, NY 10022
Fax: (212) 207-7654

Editor and texts: Daniela Santos Quartino
Art director: Mireia Casanovas Soley
Translation: Heather Bagott
Layout: Nil Solà Serra

Library of Congress Cataloging-in-Publication Data

Santos Quartino, Daniela.
 New Spas and Resorts / Daniela Santos Quartino.—1st ed.
 p. cm.
 ISBN 13: 978-0-06-114998-6 (hardcover)
 ISBN 10: 0-06-114998-5 (hardcover)
 1. Hotels.   2. Hotels—Decoration.   3. Interior architecture—History—20th
century.   4. Interior architecture—History—21st century.   I. Title: New hotels
three.   II. Title.

NA7800.N493 2007
910.46'09'0511—dc22
2005034966

Printed in China

First Printing, 2007

8 | Introduction

10 | Day and Fitness Spas

12 | Granny.M
20 | Bloww
26 | Studio W
34 | Edge Lotus
40 | Xel-Ha
48 | Wonderland
54 | Duet Tiana
62 | Sportplaza Mercator

70 | Hotel Spas

72 | The Standard
82 | Spa Caudalie at the Marqués de Riscal Hotel
94 | The Ritz Carlton Spa
100 | Sámas Spa
106 | Ten Spa
116 | Ahín Wellness & Spa
124 | The Peninsula Spa
134 | SpaciOmm
142 | SPOT Remota
150 | Botta's Bergoase

162 | Thermal Spas

164 | Blue Lagoon
174 | Merano Thermal Baths
182 | Onsen Retreat and Spa
188 | NOVA Köflach Thermal Spa
196 | Geométricas Thermal Spa
204 | Thermae Bath Spa

214 | Unique Spas

216 | Aman-i-Khás
220 | Sea Sauna
226 | Harnn Heritage Spa
230 | Winter Bath at Spree River
240 | Cowshed at Clarendon Cross
244 | Dolce & Gabbana Beauty Farm
250 | Cowshed Spa at the Virgin Atlantic ClubHouse

254 | Resorts

256 | Uma Paro
264 | W Retreat & Spa
274 | Earth Spa
282 | Porto Elounda Deluxe Resort
290 | Zeavola
298 | One&Only Reethi Rah
304 | Kempinski Hotel Barbaros Bay
314 | COMO Shambhala Estate
326 | Bulgari Resort

334 | Directory

Introduction

The growing popularity of spas is a phenomenon that will become more pronounced and innovative, according to experts in the field. Access to these well-being centers has ceased to be a luxury and has almost become a near-necessity, thanks to the rich diversity of choices now. Moreover, spas are moving from their traditional settings in isolated locations and are being in sports clubs, medical centers, airports, shopping centers, and beauty salons. Hotels are using this sector to promote their image and attract new clients. In fact, guests at hotels with wellness centers, stay longer and spend more, compared to establishments without such facilities.

Spas offer yet another reason to travel. The chance to disconnect from daily life and experience new rituals linked to cultures in faraway lands is a good reason to catch a plane and stay 10 or 15 days in a therapeutic center. Even couples are choosing a spa stay for their honeymoon or for a romantic getaway when they can enjoy indulgent treatments together.

At the other end of the scale, day spas are also gaining impetus, offering one-hour treatments or morning programs to revitalize the body, renew energies, or reduce stress.

Fusion is the common denominator for spa treatments: Thai massages (stretching, yoga, and massages), watsu (shiatsu in the pool), wellness (beauty and gym programs), jacuzzi with chromotherapy, sauna and music therapy are just some examples of the indulgences on the menu.

However, the most important ingredient is the idea that gave birth to the wellness culture. The word spa is an acronym for the Latin phrase *sanus per aquam,* which means health through water. Water connects people with their most intimate self and helps them reach emotional and physical equilibrium, through the relaxing power of water in hydrotherapy and the showers of tropical rain and sea fog, or through seawater's healing properties in thalassotherapy and natural thermal waters.

Day and Fitness Spas

In the search for physical beauty, surreal settings
and extraordinary environments have been created
as an escape from the reality of our daily lives.

Granny.M

Toyokawa, Japan

The image of a brick house with a triangular-shaped roof is a familiar sight in nearly any culture. Such a simple shape enhances the concept of a home built according to the rules set by the owners themselves.

The two treatment rooms are decorated with rectangular-shaped ceramic tiles and take their inspiration from this idea. According to their creator, the architect Hiroyuki Miyake, "a scene of fiction with a touch of nostalgia, not dissimilar to a fairy story, has been created."

The first of the rooms runs along the window at the front of the building and attracts attention from outside. It is an access tunnel that takes you to a new reality of different proportions and shapes. Another, larger room, built in the interior the salon, houses the washing and relaxation area and has a more intimate feel. The decor of the styling and cutting area, is framed by a kind of spacious and luminous courtyard, surrounded by sizable mirrors and provincial-style seating. The warmth of the wood and the traditional style of the chairs provide a more familiar look in a space that is at once stylish and fascinating.

Opening date: 2005
Photography: © Nacása & Partners

Services
Beauty salon, hairdressers

Web
www.granny.co.jp

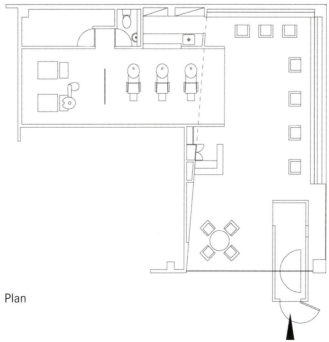

Plan

The ceramic tiles were designed especially for the treatment rooms and evoke a brick wall with more than 10 different colors of brick.

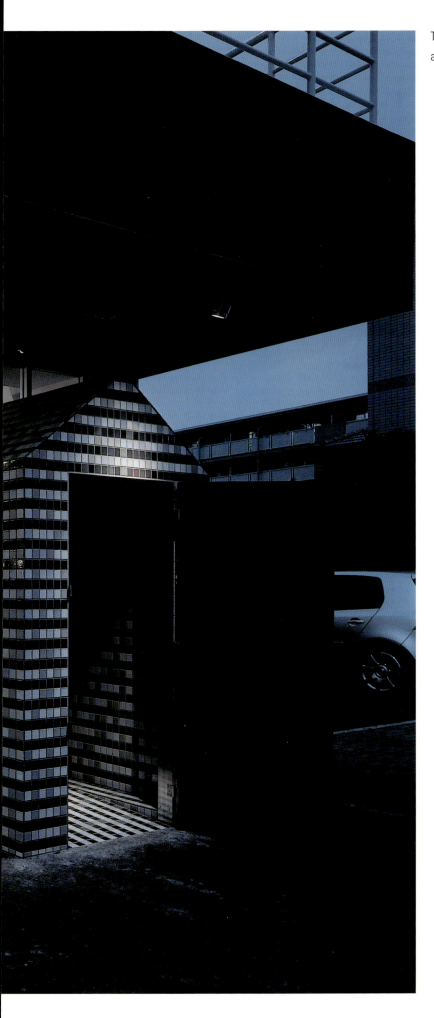

Bloww

London, United Kingdom

Bloww aims to be more than just a simple beauty salon, although "superlative modern hairstyling" is something at which they excel. Under the maxim "look good and feel good," the salon also offers relaxation and revitalization treatments.

Light is an essential element in defining the ambience that fills the space. A lighting system of varying intensity that simulates natural light has been used in place of spotlights. There are two music channels, one for the salon and one for the treatment sector.

The beauty and well-being area are connected on the lower level of the space. There, each one of seven treatment rooms holds special beds and tables, such as a wet-stone therapy table, a flotation therapy room, and an oriental steam room.

The result is an establishment that re-creates the spirit of the area where its located in between the bohemian chic of Soho and the elegance of Regent Street. It is the coexistence of sobriety and modern decor that gives the salon its stamp of originality.

Opening date: 2005
Photography: © Carlos Domínguez

Services
Hairdressers, beauty treatments

Web
www.bloww.com

The modern furniture brings color to a background that features neutral colors to induce relaxation.

Studio W

São Paulo, Brazil

This beauty salon, which is housed on the top floor of a well-known São Paulo shopping center, owes its identity to what at first seemed to be a serious obstacle—the metal beams that run along the area diagonally from floor to roof in the area where shops used to store their inventory.

The architects transformed the beams into an asset, and the w-shaped steel structures were endowed with aesthetic importance. Not only were they painted green, making them stand out from the rest of the area, but the space was actually organized around them.

The result is an elegant salon with an industrial feel that has space for up to 120 clients at any one time. The decor and luxe furniture bring warmth to the atmosphere of the waiting room and sitting area near the entrance. Abundant natural light flows freely around its 5,458 square feet of space. A section of the ceiling in glass an floor-to-ceiling windows link the space to the exterior.

Opening date: 2005
Photography: © Tuca Reinés

Services
Hairdressers

Web
www.studiow.com.br

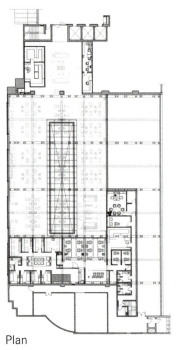
Plan
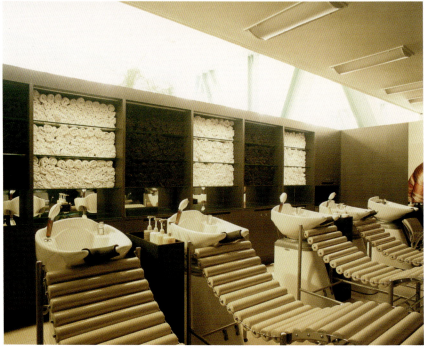

The large metal beams that provide the shopping center's structural support give Studio W its identity.

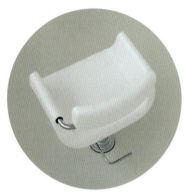

Edge Lotus

Kuwana, Japan

A world away from the usual mirrors and chairs lined up along a wall, Edge Lotus offers a new concept where the privacy of clients comes first. An ingenious partition of the space allows this to happen.

The architect, Hiroshi Nakamura, utilizes several winding curls that divide the salon into 24 interconnected circular modules. In this way, the partitions are organic, created by curved walls that reach a maximum height of 4.5 feet and leave the upper part of the salon open—to maintain a serene, airy atmosphere.

When greater privacy is desired, some translucent organdy curtains can be closed. These co-exist alongside delicate steel columns and a ceiling made of a fine, perforated metal.

The slope of the floor, which descends gradually from the entrance to the end of the salon, enables the walls to assume different functions depending on their height—from reception desk, to waiting chairs and exhibition cases.

The pastel colors blend the walls with the floor, blurring the limits between these planes and reinforcing a feeling of fluidity and weightlessness that dominates in this space dedicated to beauty.

Opening date: 2006
Photography: © Nobuaki Nakagawa, NAP Architects

Services
Beauty salon, hairdressers

Web
www.edge-hair.com

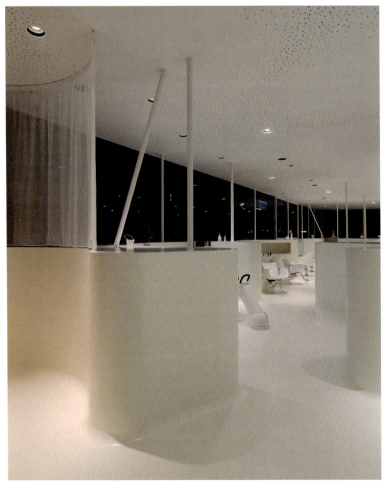

Each space has a 4-foot radius, which enables the professionals to move comfortably around the client.

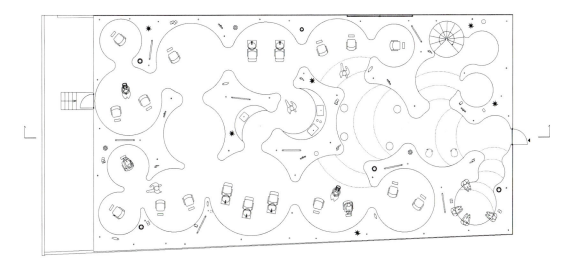

Plan

Xel-Ha

Tokyo, Japan

When Jun Aoki received the job of designing this beauty salon, the ceiling was one of the few places where the architects could leave their mark. In fact, because it is so visible from the outside, this 3.746 square-foot-ceiling has become the signature element of this building in Omotesando, the most fashionable neighborhood of the Japanese capital.

In Xel-Ha by Afloat, the ceiling consists of a special lighting system involving spiral sheets of plastic washi, a material that works as an excellent diffuser of light. It is traditionally used in Japan to make lamps. In this case, each one of the tubes covers a round-shaped fluorescent lamp. As a result, the light source is on show without being uncomfortable to look at.

According to the architect, "a salon should be a little theatrical as well as comfortable." In Xel-Ha, the ethereal ceiling evokes a large cloud above a landscape of dark browns and stainless steel furniture. This color scheme is maintained throughout the right wing of the establishment, where the rooms for body and facial treatments are housed.

Opening date: 2005
Photography: © Daici Ano

Services

Hairdressers, body and facial beauty treatments

Web

www.afloat.co.jp

The ceiling of the salon is the most visible element from the outside—especially at night, when it assumes the appearance of a floating cloud.

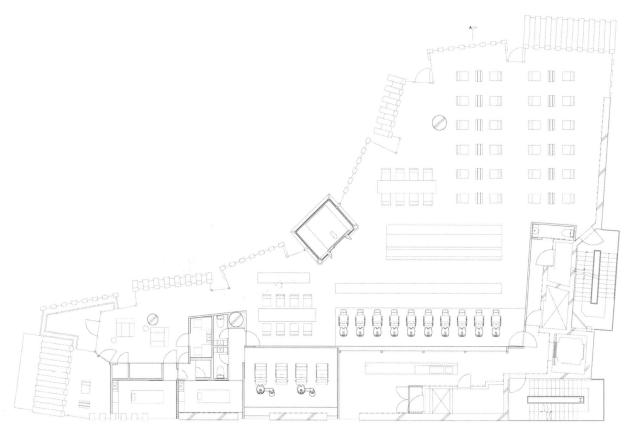

Plan

Wonderland

New York, USA

Wonderland is located in the very heart of the New York City's fashionable Meatpacking District, and the name is a salute to the eclectic, fun, and original aesthetic of this salon. Every inch has been designed to surprise, from the varnished cement floor, which shines like the streets of New York at night, to the stuffed leopard in the doorway, which welcomes the salon's A-list clients. At the entrance, a deep-pink neon sign resting on a bed of 1,600 silk flowers planted in the wall, reveals the name of the salon. The reception area contains an impressive glass chandelier, which hangs over the desk covered in tufted pink vinyl.

The workstations in the styling area have been fixed onto a metal container and boast translucent chairs by Phillipe Starck. Venetian-glass mirrors hang from metal pipes, thus bringing the films that are projected onto the back wall into view (among them, La Dolce Vita, Edward Scissorhands, and Beauty and the Beast).

The scenery changes radically in the bathrooms, where the paint on the walls and ceilings simulates a circus tent. The changing rooms adjacent to the clothes-and-curiosities shop are again different and made of recycled wooden slats with a screen covered in fluorescent wall paper.

The intense illumination—vital for hair-coloring work—imitates natural light. The more than 34,000 songs that make up the soundtrack to this beauty salon are the final touch to an environment based on fun.

Opening date: 2005
Photography: © Michael Angelo

Services
Beauty salon, hairdressers

Web
www.wonderlandbeautyparlor.com

Wonderland draws on sources of inspiration as diverse as Madonna, Paul Smith, Walt Disney, and the photographers Pierre et Gilles.

Duet Tiana

Barcelona, Spain

Simple and seemingly sealed from the outside, this local sports club is brightly colored and full of natural light inside.

Located in an area of parking lots and football fields, the building of Alonso Balaguer presents a design of formal simplicity. The club consists of two metal boxes on top of a concrete base, where the most important activities are carried out.

An open-air terrace visually connects the fitness and spinning rooms with the spacious water zone consisting of an indoor pool, thermal pools, saunas, and Turkish baths, as well as a pool specifically for back therapy, with water jets and waterfalls.

So as not to distort the box idea, the long windows are minimum incisions in the facade walls. At the same time, they guarantee that club members always have visual contact with the spectacular sea and mountain views.

Inside, a world of letters, images, and vibrant color fills the space, from the changing rooms to the doors. The signage on the walls of different areas and near various activities is a distinctive feature and becomes an architectural element that stimulates dynamism and vitality in a center dedicated to well-being.

Opening date: 2005
Photography: © Josep M. Molinos

Services
Swimming pools, thermal pools, saunas, fitness area, spinning, solarium

Web
www.duetsports.com

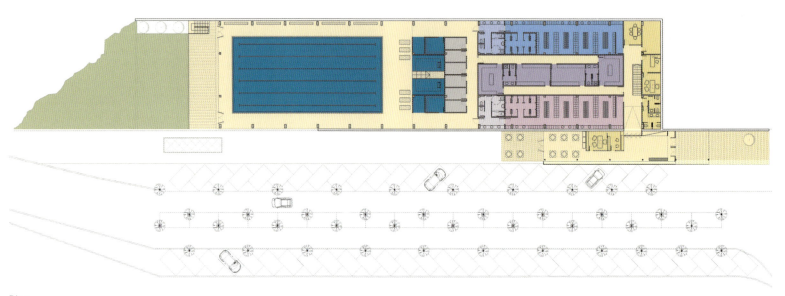

Plan

The use of strong colors reinforces the dynamics of the activities areas.

Sportplaza Mercator

Amsterdam, Holland

The facade of this new urban sports center supports a variety of vegetation, which over time will resemble a green cloak of trees, bushes, and all kinds of plants. From above, the building changes color in harmony with the seasons and blends into its setting.

From the side, the building looks as though it is emerging from the ground, and the green curtain covering it reveals a changing interior world—observable through the irregular openings in the vegetation growing over the real windows.

The entrance to the sports center is similar to an airport entrance, with its transparent-glass elevators and hanging corridors, where visitor can enjoy views over the entire complex of fitness suites, sauna, swimming pools, a bar, and a large area for parties. The indoor pools are connected together at weekends and become one enormous mirror of water with various areas for relaxation or for simply watching the proceedings.

At night, when the only lights left on are those underwater, the ceiling is transformed into a sky full of stars over a seemingly infinite sea.

Opening date: 2006
Photography: © Luuk Kramer

Services
Sauna, swimming, fitness

Web
www.sportplazamercator.nl

Fitness areas, saunas, and hydrotherapy pools are the core activities in this complex, which is surrounded by nature in the heart of Amsterdam.

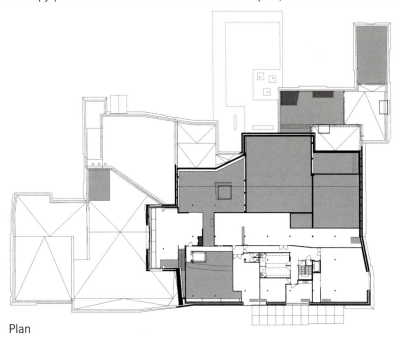

Plan

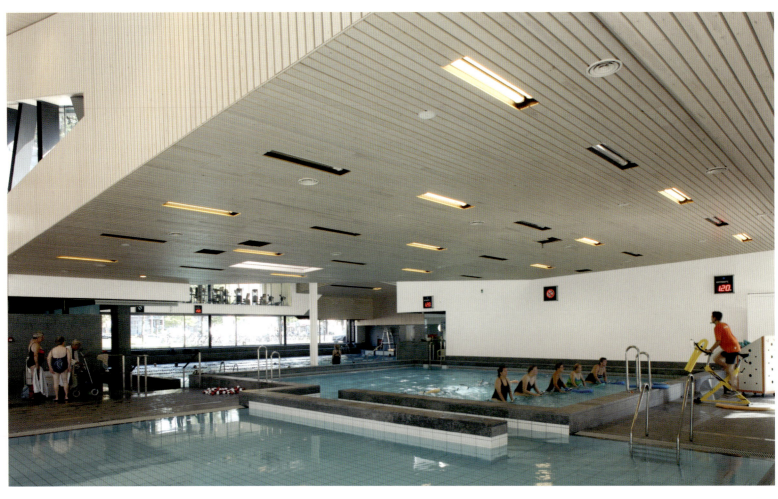

Hotel Spas

Focusing on a new concept of personal care, hotels are
promoting their image through in-house spaces
for relaxation and beauty therapy, which they offer
to guests and nonresidents.

The Standard

Miami, USA

In this spa-hotel on Belle Isle in Biscayne Bay, the philosophy is somewhat unexpected. Quite the opposite of the majority of today's spas, which are focused on individual therapies, The Standard promotes communal treatments, as in Roman times, when the spa was a place for relaxation, exercise, socializing, and intellectual stimulation.

The spa rooms are based on this premise, such as the space where guests can cover themselves and others with mud rich in mineral properties.

The whole of the third floor of the hotel is devoted to hydrotherapy, including Turkish baths, aroma steam rooms and scrub rooms, a cedar sauna, and a sound shower room with speakers that reproduce the sound of small waterfalls or the wind blowing through the trees, or just play rock and roll. Outside, there is a Roman waterfall hot tub, an Arctic plunge pool, a sound pool with an underwater sound system, along with various pools of different shapes and sizes—all with hydrotherapy.

A large number of the treatments are DIY (do it yourself) which increases awareness them and reduces the cost of the facilities, which are also on offer to nonresidents.

Opening date: 2006
Photography: © Nikolas Koenig-Ken Hayden

Services

Hydrotherapy, steam baths, sauna, holistic therapies, beauty treatments

Web

www.standardhotel.com

A large number of the treatments are DYI (do it yourself).

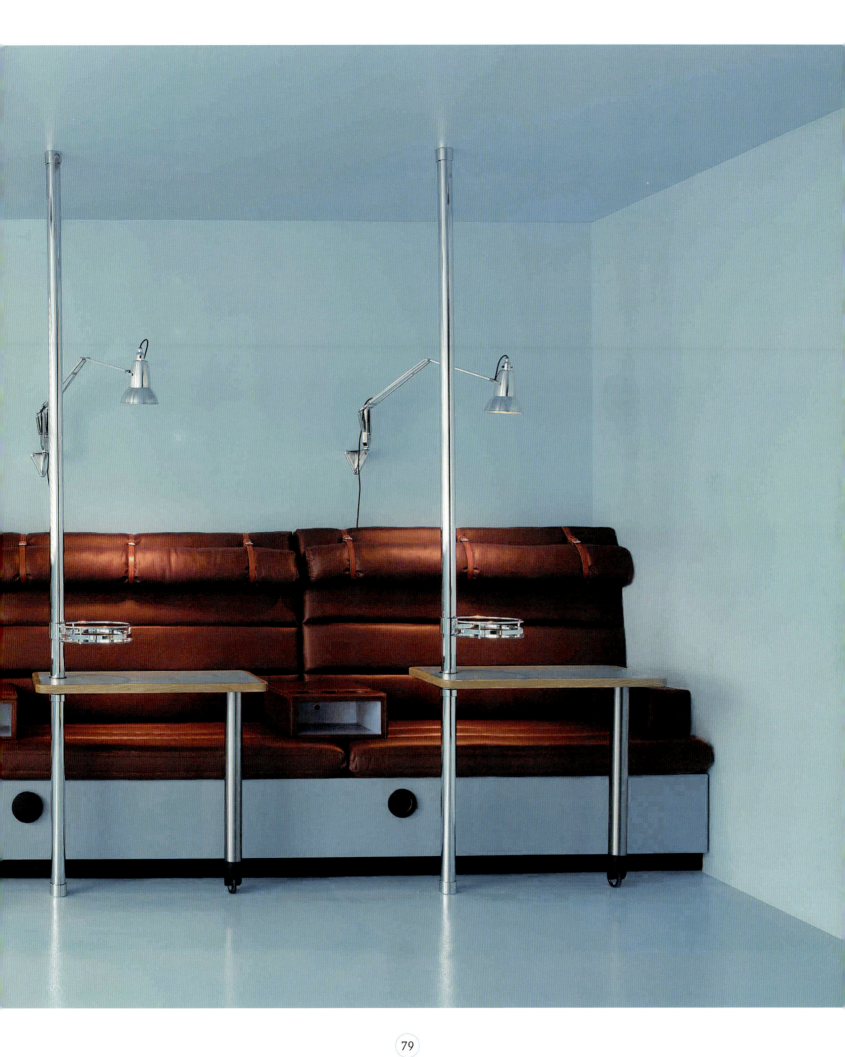

The spa's Scandinavian style of decor is akin to saunas; however, the spirit of Florida comes through in the contrasting color schemes.

Spa Caudalie at the Marqués de Riscal Hotel

Elciego, Spain

This spa devoted to wine therapy is located in Rioja Alavesa, one of the most prestigious red wine regions of Spain. Wine therapy is one of the newest wellness fields, and it profits from the many revitalizing qualities of the grape.

Housed in an annex of the Marqués de Riscal Hotel, in Spain's so-called City of Wine, the spa is part of an enological complex designed by Frank Gehry among the vineyards near the medieval village of Elciego.

The materials and shapes used by the architect in this Luxury Collection hotel are reminiscent of the Guggenheim Museum in Bilbao, although here the titanium covering the structure has been dyed wine inspired colors.

The spa, which is run by the originators of wine treatment, Caudalie, is housed in an annex connected to the hotel by a corridor. It boasts an indoor pool, Turkish baths, barrel baths, Jacuzzi, invigorating showers, a fitness zone, and fourteen beauty treatment rooms. The programs blend the benefits of mineral-rich thermal waters with grape and wine extracts rich in polyphenols, which slows the aging process. There are also baths and wraps using red-grape extracts and essential organic oils and massages with extra-fine grapeseed oil, which nourishes and smoothes the skin.

Just like a young fresh wine, the intense red color that dominates the interior design of the spa evokes the antioxidant and regenerating effects of the grape, the chief character of this dramatic complex which blends gastronomy, hotel accommodation, and well-being treatments.

Opening date: 2006
Photography: Adrian Tyler, Rodolphe Cellier
© Marqués de Riscal Hotel, the Luxury Collection

Services
Wine therapy, fitness center

Web
www.marquesderiscal.com

The spa offers wine therapy treatments in an annex of the building designed by Frank Gehry.

Sketch

The programs blend the benefits of mineral-rich thermal waters with grape and wine extracts.

Wine and grape colors are used in the interior design.

The Ritz Carlton Spa

Laguna Niguel, USA

Situated halfway between Los Angeles and San Diego on a cliff top 148-feet above sea level, the Ritz Carlton Laguna Niguel provides the ideal setting for its recently renovated and expanded spa.

The sensory experience begins as soon as you go through the glass curtain to the lobby decorated with marble mosaics. Continue along the corridor leading to the 11 therapy rooms and you'll find sparkling chandeliers.

Here, water is without a doubt the key aspect, not only in many of the treatments, but also as an artistic element in sculpture with water jets at the entrance to the spa, and in the mini waterfalls throughout the installation.

In addition to the sauna, the Vichy showers—a combination of relaxing manual massage with thermal-water showers—and the steam baths, the spa also offers exclusive treatments to revitalize the body. One of these is the application of collagen, which deeply nourishes the facial epidermis; another is the herbal-infusion massage, which is meant to reduce tension. The center also offers body exfoliation made from Californian fruits, which helps regenerate cells; the Ashiatsu massage—originally used in the Buddhist monasteries—enhances structural rejuvenation.

Physical activities include tennis, golf, Yoga, Tai-chi, Pilates, and a luxury fitness suite with privileged Ocean Pacific views.

Opening date: 2005
Photography: © Fred Licht

Services

Sauna, massages, hydrotherapy, beauty and health treatments, manicure/pedicure, fitness

Web

www.ritzcarlton.com

The fitness room boasts multimedia equipment and is at the front of the building, where there are with great sea views.

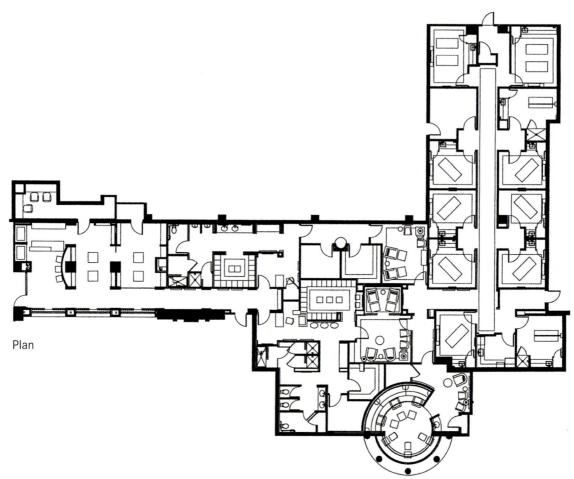

Plan

Sámas Spa

Kenmare, Ireland

The Sámas Spa is set in the idyllic landscape of the Ring of Kerry located on the west coast of Ireland, where stories of fairies and gnomes abound. The journey towards purification begins with the sound of water cascading down one of the walls in the hallway, which joins the modern spa with the manorial building of Park Hotel Kenmare.

The infinite woods, which prevail through the glass walls, shelter the visitor as they pass through the hotel's reception area. The treatments carried in the thermal suites, relaxation rooms and meditation areas are complemented with views over Kenmare Bay. In addition, the site has gardens with private pools as well as a main pool which seems to flow over into the surrounding landscape.

With the help of local natural materials such as wood and stone, glass walls which blur the limits with the surroundings and a grass roof, this building perfectly transforms into a temple of nature and relaxation destined exclusively to pleasing the senses, as its name suggests in Gaelic.

Opening date: 2003
Photography: © Sámas Spa

Services
Heat features, outdoor Vitality Pool, holistic treatments

Web
www.samaskenmare.com

A three-hour route takes you through all the treatment rooms—the sauna, the relaxation area and the swimming pool.

Ten Spa

Winnipeg, Canada

When designer Belinda Albo began planning the spa that would encompass the entire tenth floor of the Hotel Fort Garry, she already knew that the style of this new space would be very different from the opulent château in which it is housed.

She, therefore, decided to design something in harmony with the elegance, that characterizes the hotel, but to maintain a modern perspective with simple lines, large white sofas, and minimalist ambiences.

The exception was the modern reinterpretation of Roman and Turkish steam baths in an area decorated in white marble, with traditional style fountains and blue mosaics. In this hamam, the treatments offered are identical to those in Roman and Turkish baths, such as exfoliation with salt or olive soap and rinsing with water that falls over the body from a bowl.

The remaining therapies are carried out in rooms where the color white prevails. These include up to nine types of facial treatments, moisturizing and nourishing treatments for the skin, and body cocoons treatments where the body is wrapped up and rests on a special envelopment bed to create a weightless sensation of dry floating.

The spacious and comfortable beds situated in the rest lounge are available for guests who wish to have a nap on linen sheets amid flowing semitransparent veils, thus completing a day devoted to recharging energies and reducing stress.

Opening date: 2006
Photography: © Tyrone McFadden

Services
Turkish baths, massages, body and facial beauty treatments

Web
www.tenspa.ca

Exclusive treatments with light and aromas and tropical mist showers make this spa an activation zone for the senses.

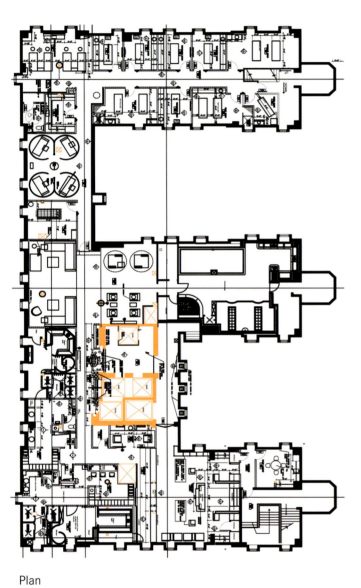

Plan

The spacious and comfortable beds are available for guests who wish to have a nap on linen sheets amid flowing semitransparent veils.

Ahín Wellness & Spa

Buenos Aires, Argentina

Ahín is a word from the Mapuche language meaning "a ritual ceremony carried out in honor of a visitor." The spa of the Park Hyatt is thus named in honor of the people who originally lived in the south-central zone of Argentina and Chile and have provided inspiration for many of the available therapies in that region.

The nature of the treatments changes over the course of the day: energizing in the morning, balancing during the day, and relaxing at night. The programs include massages and body and facial beauty applications.

The 2,400-square-foot square spa boasts a semi-Olympic indoor pool, and five spa suites for holistic treatments, including a hydrotherapy suite or Vichy shower, two individual suites, and two spa suites with hydromassage. There is also a cutting-edge gymnasium that is available to guests 24 hours a day. In harmony with the atmosphere of the Palacio Duhau houses the hotel, the spa is an elegant and luxurious space without excesses, featuring wooden and travertine marble finishes and beveled-glass details on the doors and windows. The relaxing water elements, the abundant natural light, and the views over the interior courtyards create an oasis of peace where guests find refuge from the bustle of the city.

Opening date: 2005
Photography: © Virginia del Giudice

Services

Hydromassages, holistic and beauty treatments, fitness

Web

www.buenosaires.park.hyatt.com

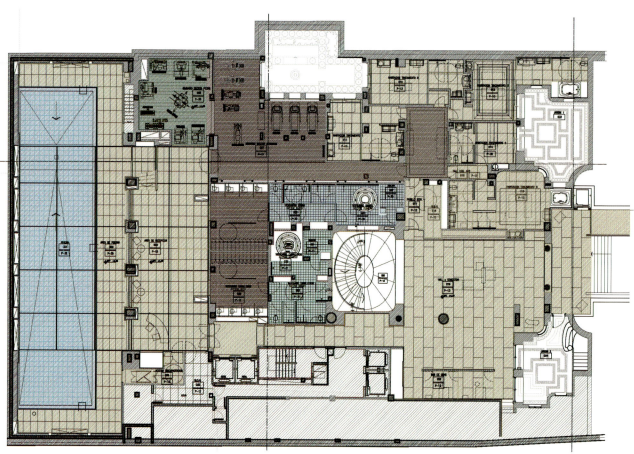

Plan

A personalized selection of music and mix of teas are prepared for each guest to accompany the treatments.

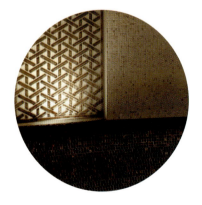

The Peninsula Spa

Kowloon, Hong Kong

Beyond the frenetic rhythm of the city, at the top of one of the towers that runs along Victoria bay, the spa at The Peninsula Hong Kong is an oasis of tranquility of Orient and Occident merge.

The spa is located on the seventh, eighth and ninth floors of the hotel. The reception, a terrace for sunbathing and the changing rooms are located on the first level. A 60-foot-long swimming pool is on the next level up, and, finally, fourteen treatment rooms, an Asian tea lounge, and a thermal suite are on the upper level.

A cup of relaxing, aromatic tea greets the visitor before entering the thermal suite, which is equipped with steam baths, aromatherapy facilities, ice fountains, showers, and saunas with spectacular harbor views.

A series of hot and cold experiences help to cleanse the skin and relax and prepare the body and mind for the rest of the treatments.

ESPA, the world's leading spa consultancy, has fused Oriental, Ayurvedic, and European therapies to create products tailored for this center. The result is a wide variety of treatments—everything from jet lag recuperation to the elimination of cellulite on hips and thighs.

The interior design blends traditional Chinese elements with modern art and technology, such as the floor-to-ceiling bamboo terrarium in the reception area and the videos of conceptual art, which are visible from the elevator and runs between the three floors comprising the spa.

Opening date: 2006
Photography: © The Peninsula Hong Kong Hotel

Services

Ayurvedic and holistic massages, body and face beauty treatments, sauna, steam baths

Web

www.peninsula.com

The interior design blends traditional Chinese elements with modern art and technology.

Each one of the relaxation beds designed for the spa boasts a personal sound system and reading lights. They are fitted with Egyptian cotton sheets.

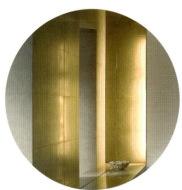

SpaciOmm

Barcelona, Spain

This wellness center at Hotel Omm could be considered a private spa offering individual programs for each person according to their emotional and physical state.

Their spa menu includes special indulgences such as the Tibetan facial treatment, a special therapy for headaches, drainage massages to overcome stress, programs with mint essences to revitalize the mind, and Ayurvedic massage using products from various countries to boost energy levels.

The thermal circuit of the spa involves an active pool with relaxation beds in the water, a waterfall, treatment jets, steam baths, ice fountains, and a therapeutic foot bath with rainwater.

There is also a gravitation space with relaxation beds that are meant to balance the organism, an experience complemented by chromotherapy and oxygen treatments.

In the "of honesty" bar, health tonics, infusions, and phototherapy-based natural juices, and a dietetic menu are available.

The space, which is open to nonresidents as well as hotel guests, also has a fitness zone and one of the foremost hairdressing salons in Barcelona, where the full complement of day spa services are on offer.

Opening date: 2006
Photography: © Lourdes Jansana, Eva Balart, Anne Soderberg, Olga Planas

Services
Ayurvedic and holistic treatments, hydrotherapy, steam baths, bar, fitness, hairdressers, beauty salon

Web
www.hotelomm.es

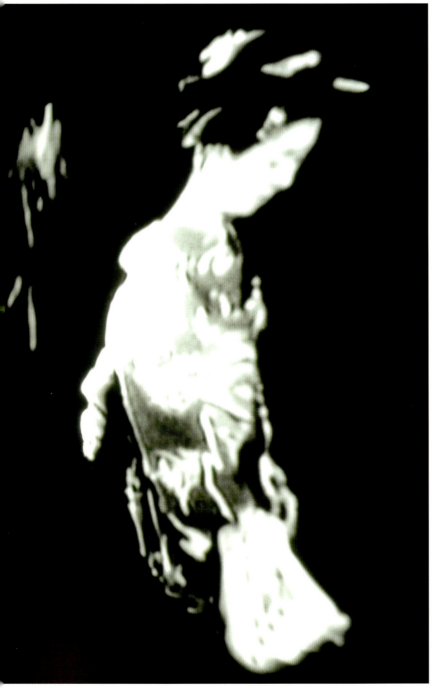

In the SpaciOmm, the pure lines create an Oriental ambience from which a large part of the available therapies draw inspiration.

SPOT Remota

Puerto Natales, Chile

The hotel Remota, located in one of the most southerly towns on the planet—the old fishing village of Puerto Natales—is the gateway to the fjords and glacial peaks of southern Chile. With the monumental Torres del Paine as a backdrop, the complex blends into its surroundings and appears slightly raised on its grassy hill overlooking the Señoret Channel. It offers spectacular views of the Patagonia.

On top of the southern wing of the building and bordering the coastline, the spa is reached by a wooden walkway. The hotel calls the facility SPOT, or *sala para el ocio total* (room for total leisure). From the temperate swimming pool, which takes up most of this wellness space, the channel below seems to merge with the pool itself through the large glass windows.

The Finnish sauna, in the same style as the pool, is furnished with distressed wood and slanting windows, reproducing the effects of the climate on buildings in this area, which are lashed by the strong winds of Patagonia and the sea salt.

The open-air Jacuzzi in this relaxation center is intended as a little corner of the world where one can keep the stresses of daily life at bay.

Opening date: 2005
Photography: © McDuff Everton

Services
Pool, Jacuzzi, sauna, massages

Web
www.remota.cl

The distressed wood and slanting windows in the pool zone evoke the Patagonian landscape.

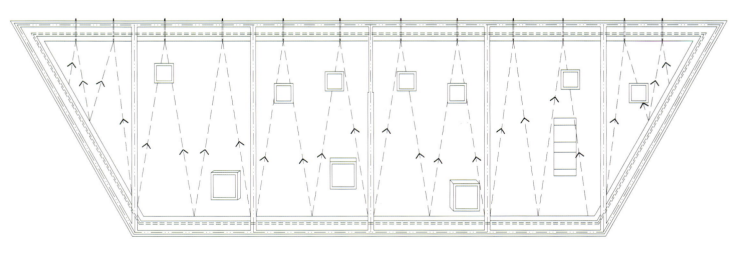

Plan

Botta's Bergoase

Arosa, Switzerland

Amid the breathtaking mountain setting of Arosa, where the struggle of man against nature is continuous, renowned architect Mario Botta created several buildings to house the spa of the Tschuggen Grand Hotel.

The landscape itself was the inspiration for the shape of the spa; the raised roof resembles a forest of trees and leaves, while the large volumes of the lower part sink into the ground.

The interior spaces are on four floors; they assume the appearance of a continual terrace following the lines of the topography with two bridges connecting them to the hotel building. The exterior spaces include an outdoor swimming pool and decks with sunbathing areas, some equipped for exercise and others for enjoying the snow.

The ground floor houses a fitness center with cutting-edge technology and changing rooms for nonresidents, who reach the installation from this level. The treatment rooms and beauty salon as well as the hydromassage pools are on the first floor. The reception and the sauna, the steam bath, and Jacuzzis "under the stars" are located on the second floor. The "aquatic world" with a swimming pool, a "mountain grotto," and more relaxation areas are situated on the third floor.

The spa enjoys a close relationship with the surrounding landscape thanks to the ample and iconic glass openings, which are the highlight of the building. These openings provide the space with abundant natural light during the day, and at night the building assumes a unique appearance—somewhere between magic and science fiction.

Opening date: 2006
Photography: © Enrico Cano, Pino Musi

Services
Sauna, hydromassage, steam baths, medical spa, beauty treatments, fitness

Web
www.tschuggen.ch

The architect, Mario Botta, created several buildings situated at the foot of the mountains to house a spa.

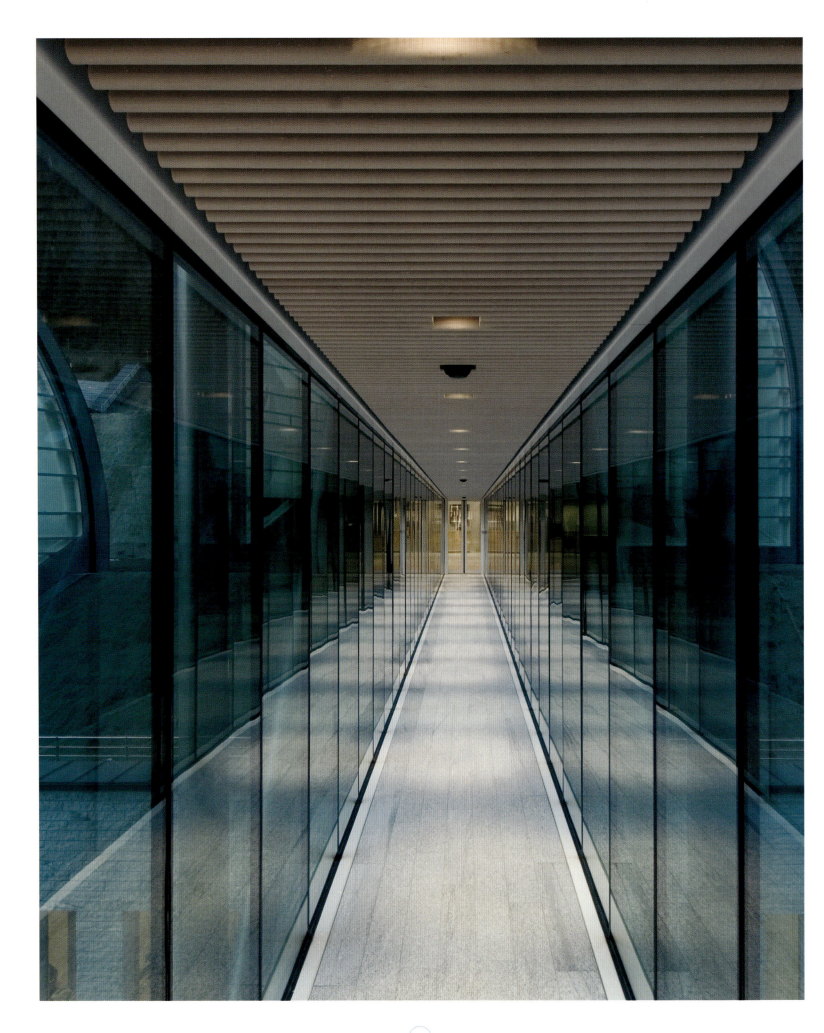

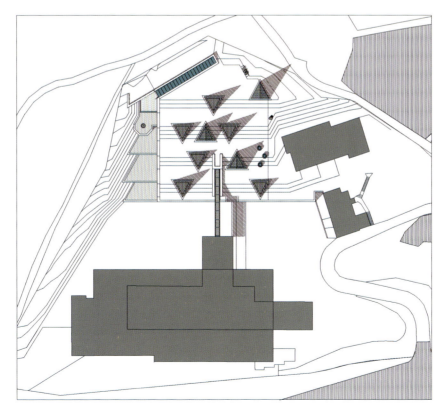

Plan

One of the exclusive spa treatments is the reproduction of climatic conditions such as summer rain, winter storms, mist, or sun in a small space.

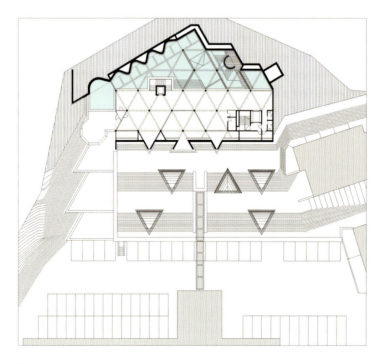

Plan

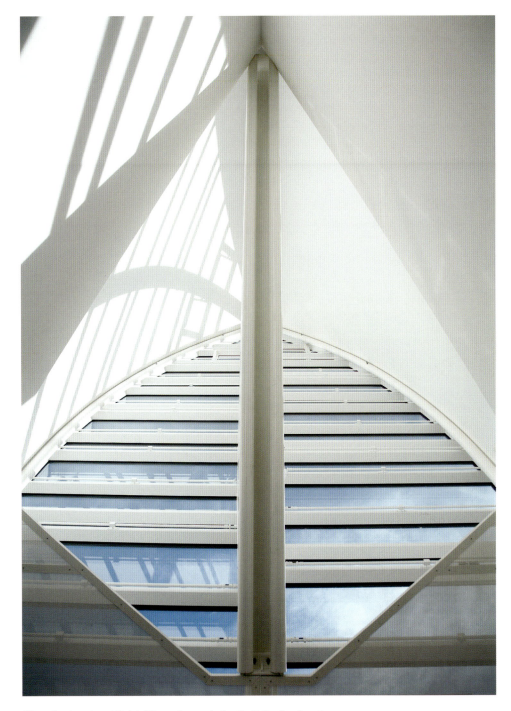

Abundant natural light filters through the building's structure.

Thermal Spas

Spaces that bring an ancient tradition back to life, thermal spas recall the beneficial health effects of hot waters that spring from the earth.`

Blue Lagoon

Svartsengi, Iceland

This geothermal spa owes its name to the intense blue color of a man-made lagoon in a millenary lava field in the southeast Iceland. Clean, warm water spills from the adjacent energy-generating plant, which brings 6 million liters to the surface every 40 hours.

On its long journey up from the depths of the earth through the porous rock mass, the liquid reaches the surface rich in minerals, algae and silica—elements that are renowned for their regenerative and curing effects.

To maximize the benefit of this wonder, a spa, a hotel, and a clinic specializing in skin treatments have been established in the heart of this geothermal area. Massages and treatments are offered in the open air on a spacious wooden platform. The indoor programs are held within the popular complex, which was designed by VA Arkitektar. The buildings incorporate saunas, steam rooms, a restaurant, and a conference room.

The design of the installations and the materials used help create a feeling of warmth in this magical place which enjoys extraordinary light and an eerily beautiful landscape.

Opening date: 2005
Photography: © Ragnar Th. Sigurdsson, Rafn Sigurdsson Oddgeir Karlsson

Services
Thermal therapies, skin clinic

Web
www.bluelagoon.com

Given the concentration of volcanoes in the area, the waters of the Blue Lagoon have extraordinary minimal content and, many say healing properties.

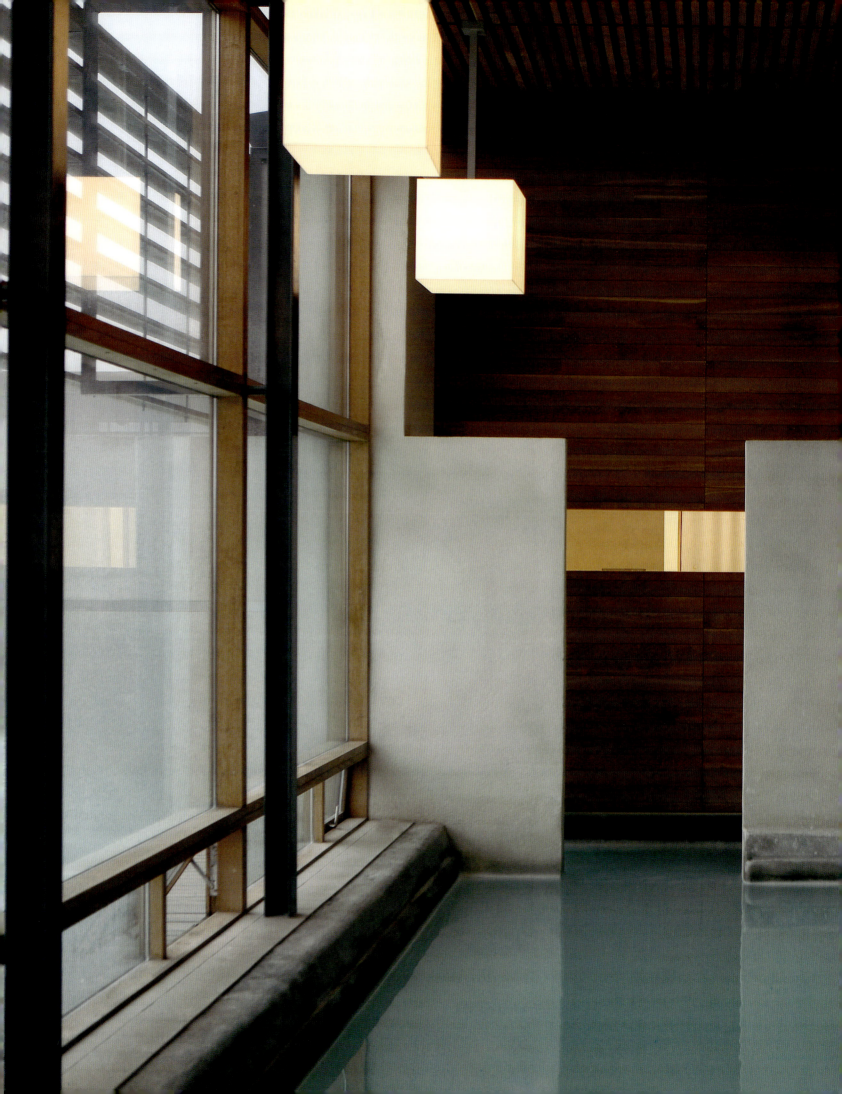

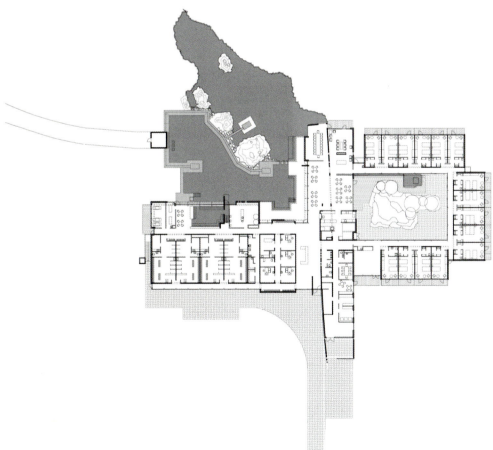

Plan

The complex houses saunas, steam rooms, a restaurant, and a conference room.

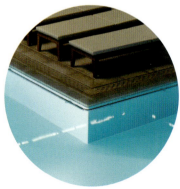

Merano Thermal Baths

Merano, Italy

The Merano Thermal Baths stand tall in an enormous steel-and-glass box in an area world famous for its spas. The center, according to the architect Matteo Thun, establishes "a nexus between the mountains and the water."

Its open structure is defined by the large space around it, which includes 13 outdoor pools, among them a swimming pool and a pool where music plays underwater. Within the transparent walls of the central building, there are twelve pools, eight saunas, twenty-six treatment rooms, and a gym. The interior of the glass box is a composition of architectural and aquatic volumes, islands, and platforms. The relaxation room and a pool for water fitness are housed in two teak box-shaped areas. The saunas, however, function in rooms acclimatized for heat and cold treatments, such as the "snow room"—a kind of gigantic cold store with artificial snowfall.

In the day spa, with its eclectic interior design and gentle lighting effects, visitors are treated to anything from baths with whey, honey, mountain hay, and sheep's wool to wine therapy, hydrotherapy, body modeling, massages, and beauty programs.

The center is in constant transformation. The Plexiglas discs and spheres that are suspended above the indoor pools fill the spaces with changing shades of light and color over the course of a day. At night, the glass box is all lit up and resembles a giant torch ablaze on the waters. A four-star hotel in the town's main square is the stunning piece de résistance of the complex.

Opening date: 2006
Photography: © Gionata Xerra

Services

Thermal swimming pools, sauna, gym, beauty salons, medical clinic, massages, hydrotherapy, hot and cold baths

Web

www.termemerano.com

The Plexiglas discs and spheres suspended above the indoor pools fill the space with changing shades of light and color.

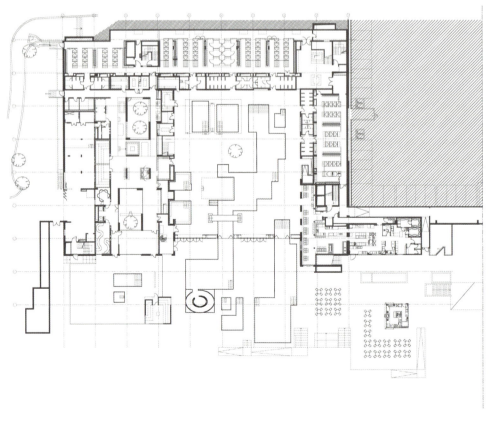

Plan

Onsen Retreat and Spa

Victoria, Australia

Dinner Plain is a homely villa which was built in 1986 in the alpine zone of Victoria, following strict architectural guidelines and a strong community spirit. The opening of the Onsen Retreat and Spa, a five-star spa joined to a leisure center and a new visitors' reception area, means tourists can enjoy the village and its facilities all year long, not just during the ski season.

The building, created in harmony with the wooded site, includes a series of paths and raised walkways where the snowy landscape can be admired.

The complex boasts a 15-meter lap pool, a gym, five treatment rooms, and an *Onsen* in the style of traditional Japanese hot-water wells filled with thermal water. There is also a restaurant and bar, a new visitors' reception area and a commercial area including a beauty salon.

The thermal water in the outdoor pool is regarded as some of the best water in Australia and reaches the surface rich in minerals after filtering through some 200 feet of decomposed granite rock. The open-air hot bath provides a revitalizing experience, especially after spending a day devoted to enjoying relaxation therapies and recharging energies.

Opening date: 2006
Photography: © Peter Bennetts

Services
Thermal waters, swimming pool, fitness, massages, beauty treatments, reiki

Web
www.onsen.com.au

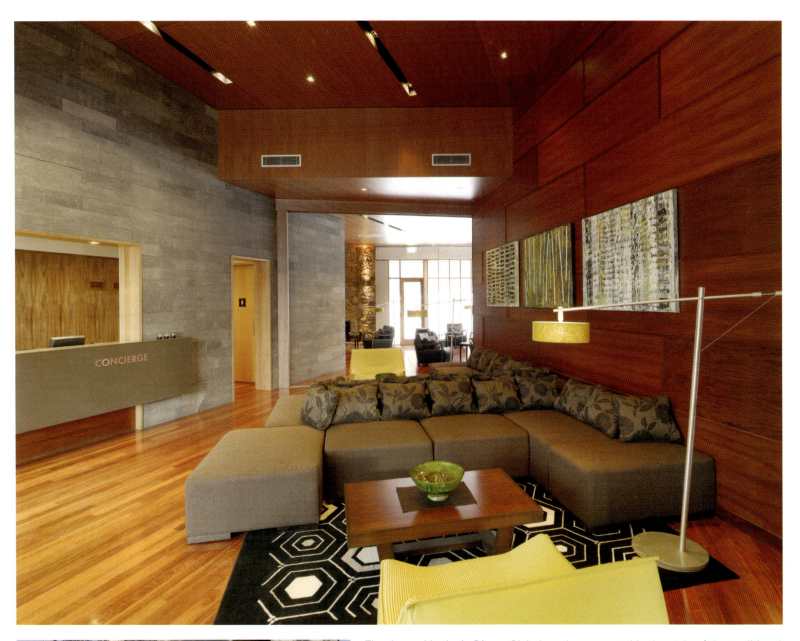

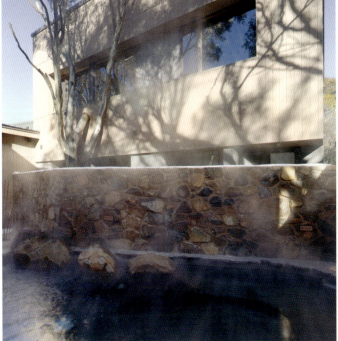

The thermal baths in Dinner Plain have been created in the style of the traditional Japanese *Onsen*.

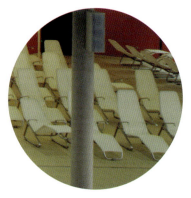

NOVA Köflach Thermal Spa

Köflach, Austria

This thermal spa and hotel in Steiermark, in southeast Austria, offer a new sensory experience, going beyond the limits of traditional therapies and crossing into new realms where there are spaces created expressly for relaxation and revitalization.

A computer program operates an installation known as "emotional illumination," in other words, the creation of ambiences using lights of different colors and brightness that radiate heat and promote a feeling of well-being. Even the abundant natural light, that flows in through the glass facade is controlled by a system of lattices modifying the way the space is perceived.

All the interior installations have a corner or virtual box in which reality assumes new shapes, thanks to lighting effects and the projection of images, sounds, and fragrances. Thus, in the tropical area, an interior garden re-creates a humid and warm climate, where there are frequent refreshing bursts of rain and paths lead to an artificial cave with steam baths.

Technology stimulates the senses continually in the underwater music system of the swimming pool, the films of the "water cinema," and the images that are projected onto a 360-degree panoramic wall in the relaxation area of the sauna.

The clever lighting seems to make the pools, which occupy two levels of this complex, transcend their physical limits and merge with the verdant landscape surrounding this futuristic thermal spa.

Opening date: 2004
Photography: © Angelo Kaunat

Services

Thermal water

Web

www.novakoeflach.at

A tower of solar light in the hall controls the lighting effects and emits different relaxing fragrances into the air.

Geométricas Thermal Spa

Villarrica National Park, Chile

These hot springs set amidst the Villarrica National Park, offer new sensations in outdoor bathing. The visitor is immersed in the cool shade of the dense surrounding forest in the summer and the snow and rain in winter.

The spa is made of more than sixty sources that produce 1.5 liters per second of thermal water at a temperature of 176-degrees Fahrenheit. The baths are taken in any of the seventeen stone wells spread along the 1,500-foot piece of land in the midst of nature. These wells and which are reached via a red-stained coihue-wood walkway.

These bathing areas vary in levels of privacy with some being more visible from the walkway than others. At night, candles are lit to show the way. When it snows, the ice melts as a result of the thermal waters; wooden canoes pass under the footbridge warmed by the water.

Each well possesses its own private changing area with forest views, toilets, and terraces for relaxation.

A simple wooden quincho (typical outdoor barbecue) has been erected halfway down the path and is an ideal spot for bathers to sit down, relax, and socialize following a dip in the waters. It is a warm sheltered area positioned around a large fire, and it makes for a perfect place to have a drink or snack or simply contemplate the silence.

Architect Germán del Sol built the center to create what he called a balance between nature and geometry, constructing it from wood and local materials in their raw state. The benefit of Geométricas, in his words, is "the primitive seduction of being purified whilst immersing oneself in hot water, or lighting a fire, or just letting oneself drift away with the monotonous and constant movement of the water that ebbs and flows and soothes."

Opening date: 2003
Photography: © Guy Wemborne

Services
Thermal baths

Web
www.termasgeometricas.cl

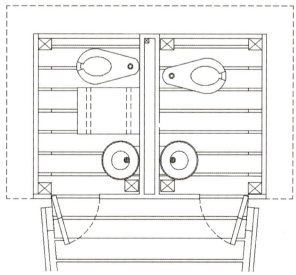

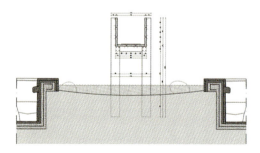

Plan

Sections

The wooden walkway is ideal for exploring the ravine and choosing a favorite bathing well.

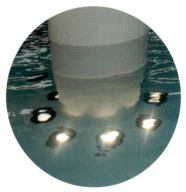

Thermae Bath Spa

Bath, United Kingdom

After closing for nearly a month, totally renovated thermal baths reopened in 2006, reinstitituting the area's ancient primacy as a thermal source. Located in the southeastern England, the World Heritage city of Bath has a long history in thermal baths. In the first century, the Romans named the area Aquae Solis (waters of the sun), however, there is some evidence that the Celts dedicated this spring to the goddess Sulis before the Romans arrived. The reopening of these baths, the only natural thermal waters in the United Kingdom, has led to the restructuring of the five existing buildings and the construction of another completely new one, the New Royal Bath. The spa houses a steam bath and aromatherapy rooms, a restaurant and café, and two swimming pools: one indoor with hydromassage and another on the roof with spectacular views over the city.

The Cross Bath, one of the baths that was restored, is an open-air thermal source that can hold only twelve people at a time. It is also where people in the past paid homage to their gods—reason enough for its status today as sacred ground.

The overall result is a complex of contrasts between antique and modern architecture, conceived as a temple where body and mind can be regenerated.

Opening date: 2006
Photography: © Matt Cardy, Edmund Sumner, Nick Smith

Services

Thermal baths, massages, regenerating treatments, and beauty treatments

Web

www.thermaebathspa.com

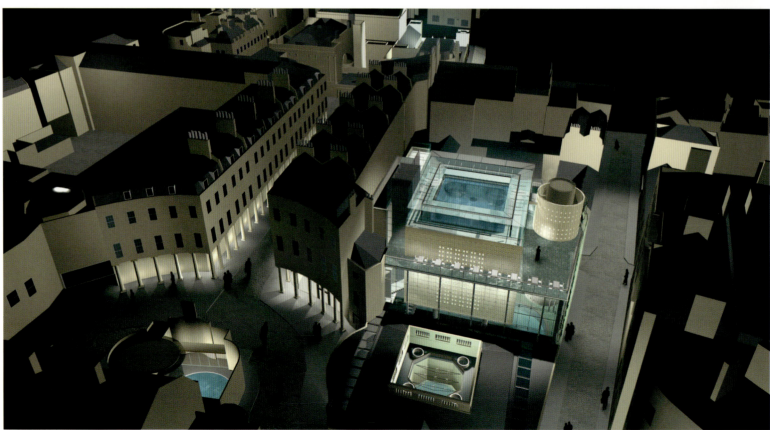

Render

With the reopening of the baths, the city of Bath has regained its ancient primacy as a thermal source.

The New Royal Bath building houses a steam bath and aromatherapy rooms, a restaurant and café, and two swimming pools.

Unique Spas

In airports, cafés, or tents, in the middle of a river, in town, or in the countryside—spas go beyond traditional locations and establish themselves in new settings.

Aman-i-Khás

Rajasthan, India

The Aman-i-Khás camp and spa lie in the heart of the Rajasthan hills, overlooking Ranthambhore National Park, today one of the most important tiger reserves in the world.

The hotel, which closes during the winter, comprises ten each tents, erected on a concrete base. Their shape emulates the ancient tents of the Mongolians in which rooms are separated with cotton sheets. One of the units is totally devoted to the spa. This room is divided into two areas, each equipped with double tables for treatments. The therapies include massages, beauty therapies such as exfoliation, wraps with hydrating and nutritive products, and foot baths. Local natural products using herbs and spices are included in all the programs.

Inspired by the traditional bawadi, a well made of concentric squares on different levels that plunge to a depth of 40 feet, serves as a pool in which to take a refreshing dip during hot summer days.

Another of the tents is devoted solely to rest. Among comfortable chairs and reading tables, there is a wide selection of books on local history and culturel, novels, magazines, and board games. The outdoor lounge is where the torches are lit every night to mark the end of another day devoted to well-being and reestablishing links with nature.

Opening date: 2003
Photography: © Amanresorts

Services
Massages and beauty treatments

Web
www.amanresorts.com/khas/home.htm

The camp includes a hotel, a spa, a restaurant, an outdoor and indoor lounge, a traditional water well, and terraces.

Sea Sauna

Stockholm, Sweden

This project inspired by a natural empathy towards the Finnish sauna—where ever experience is a pleasure—led the architect Ari Leinonen to wonder "Where would I put the ideal sauna?" The floating wooden structure she created is the answer to this recurring question "as close as possible to the water so that there is just one step between the sauna and the immersion".

The result is a sauna which is constructed depending on the needs of each user: small (for five), medium (for ten) and large (for 15).

The structure which houses this hot bath is fitted on top of a flatboat which is easy to transport to any place with access to water. All the components are made from solid wood created using lamination technology. The wood of the exterior part of the structure has been dyed black, whereas inside it has been left natural, in memory of the traditional saunas.

The structures house changing rooms, sauna rooms and showers. The sauna's sloping wall provides a very comfortable place to sit. The windows let natural light into the sauna and also provide relaxing views of the surroundings. The external shape of the structure serves as a shelter from the sea breeze after the revitalizing dip in the cold water.

Opening date: 2006
Photography: © Cia Stiernstedt, Ari Leinonen

Services
Floating sauna

Web
www.modernliving.se

A floating wooden structure in the heart of Stockholm blends tradition with modernity.

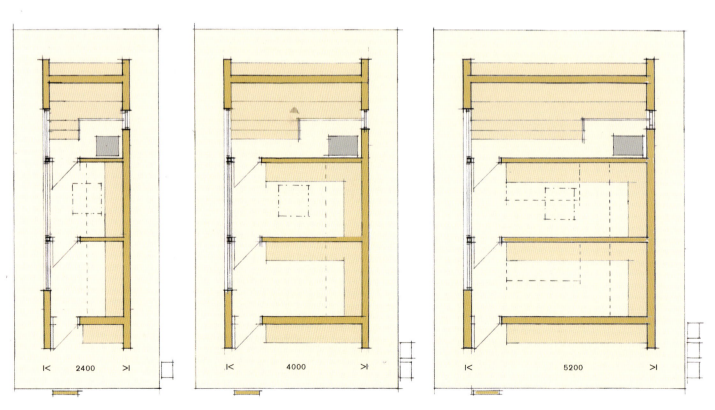

Plans

Harnn Heritage Spa

Bangkok, Thailand

The dark wood shelving that fills entire walls is reminiscent of old Chinese medicine shops. This step back in time is noticeable as soon as you cross the threshold. The use of techniques and products inspired by age-old knowledge is the foundation for this spa situated on the fourth floor of the Siam Paragon shopping center.

The Harnn shop, which sells natural products, occupies the hall leading to the treatment rooms of the establishment.

The body therapy rooms are fully equipped with tubs and private showers. Their soft light, revitalizing aromas, and relaxing music create a perfect setting for the massages, stretching, acupuncture, hot compresses, and herbal deep-cleansing programs for the skin. The principal objective of all the treatments is to eliminate tension and improve circulation so that the body can heal itself by strengthening its immune system.

The reflexology massage rooms have a softer lighting system, whereas the Thai massage rooms are more spacious and brighter and are decorated with antiques which give testament to centuries of great Asian wisdom regarding health practices.

Opening date: 2005
Photography: © Jessada Chartmontri

Services
Massages, acupuncture, body cleansing and revitalizing programs, and a health products shop

Web
www.harnn.com

One of the exclusive treatments of this spa is sesame-seed exfoliation, which smoothes, nourishes, and revitalizes the skin.

Winter Bath at Spree River

Berlin, Germany

Berlin possesses an island for relaxation and well-being on the river Spree. The futuristic facility works during the winter with two saunas and an indoor pool where guests can enjoy panoramic views of the city while sheltering from the winter cold.

At the beginning of the twentieth century, a dozen or more swimming pools bordered this river, which flows through the city center. However, progressively worse pollution and its negative effects on health led to the disappearance of these urban baths. Paying homage to this tradition, the hull of a cargo boat was fitted out in order to house a 240-square-meter, 2-meter-deep swimming pool that opens in the summer months. For the winter, architects Gil Wilk and Thomas Freiwald created a collapsible frame of steel and wood on top of the pool and access bridge. The structure is covered with a fine membrane that covers three different spaces: the lounge, the sauna, and the water zone.

The series of translucent and semitransparent membranes permit constant views of the outside. Whether seen from the chaise longues in the saunas or from the bar while having an invigorating drink, Berlin's vibrant city center always displays on this unusual wellness retreat.

Opening date: 2005
Photography: © Torsten Seidel, Arena Berlin, Gil Wilk

Services

Sauna and pool on the river Spree

Web

www.arena-berlin.de

Two saunas, a pool, and a bar comprise a center for relaxation on the river, in the heart of Berlin.

The hull of a cargo boat was fitted out in order to house a 240-square-meter swimming pool with a depth of 2 meters.

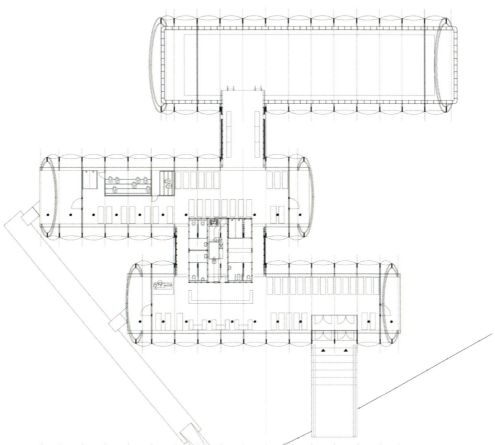

Plan

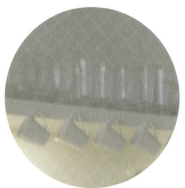

Cowshed at Clarendon Cross

London, United Kingdom

Café or day spa? How about both? This center is somewhere to meet friends for a coffee or a light snack and indulge oneself in relaxing beauty treatments. The Cowshed is located in a Georgian house in Notting Hill. There is an open-plan kitchen on the first level, as well as the pedicure-manicure zone and a small shop in the reception area selling the brand's natural products.

Fresh juices, milkshakes, teas and coffees are just some of the offerings on the menu, which includes more substantial dishes at lunch, such as soups, salads, and sandwiches. The white leather chairs are perfect for relaxing while an expert is working on your hands. The facial and body treatment rooms are in the basement, where the natural-wood walls contrast with the pure-white resin floor. The leather seats, each one with its own plasma screen for watching DVDs, are where the facial treatments for both men and women are done.

The body massages, waxing, and wraps take place in a separate room where the solarium is also located.

The interior design by the firm Ilse Crawford is similar to that of the Cowshed in the exclusive SoHo House in New York and features a modern, yet rustic style, with simple lines and warm touches, thanks to the use of materials such as wood and leather.

Opening date: 2005
Photography: © Cowshed

Services

Restaurant, bar, beauty treatments, massages, UV sun bed

Web

www.cowshedclarendoncross.com

The open-plan kitchen (opposite top) with 10 wooden dining tables welcomes visitors as soon as they enter the Georgian building in Notting Hill.

Dolce & Gabbana Beauty Farm

Milan, Italy

Under the auspices of the fashion designers, Dolce & Gabbana, a Renaissance Milanese palazzo re-creates an exclusively masculine environment. A traditional Sicilian barber's shop, a beauty farm, and a modern Martini bar share with the brand shop a space that contrasts old and new.

A large dark-grey basalt staircase, created by the architect David Chipperfield, stands at the entrance to No. 15 Corso Venezia St.

In the midst of black velvet seats and screens showing the firm's fashion shows, the first two floors are reserved for showing off the season's fashion collections and accessories.

Baroque-style chairs, cactus plants in basalt pots, Sicilian jugs, black glass walls, and original seventeenth-century artwork all coexist within Ferruccio Laviani's interior design.

In a setting dominated by green marble, walnut and chestnut, the barbers in their shop offer a traditional shave under the light of an impressive Murano chandelier. The beauty farm, however, is a more minimalist space decorated in Carrara marble. The six rooms, specially designed to enhance intimacy, offer a menu of masculine beauty treatments and programs to eliminate stress.

Opening date: 2003
Photography: © Andrea Martiradonna

Services
Masculine spa, barbers, shop, bar

Web
www.dolcegabbana.it

The contrasts inherent in of Dolce & Gabbana garments are also evident in the minimalist beauty farm (above and opposite) and traditional style of the Sicilian barbershop (pages 248 and 249).

Cowshed Spa at the Virgin Atlantic ClubHouse

Heathrow Airport, London, United Kingdom

What a great idea to build a spa in an airport so that passengers can avoid agonizing waits and overcome the effects of jet lag or pre-flight nerves.

The spa and salon Cowshed operates in the terminal area at of Heathrow is part of the Virgin Atlantic ClubHouse, a complex designed by the architects Softroom. It includes a restaurant, a café, a cocktail bar, a multiscreen cinema, a board game zone, a video game room, and a library.

Hidden behind the water wall in the center of the club are the "pampering rooms," a curved space decorated with shiny black mosaics. In this area, passengers can pamper themselves, choosing from treatments as varied as facial relaxation, shoulder massage, manicures-pedicures, and a wet shave for men. Each room is equipped with a massage chair and enough space for two therapists to work with each client. Whoever needs an improved tan can try a sun session in the St. Tropez shower.

The relaxation area houses six steam-shower rooms—each decorated in a different color of glass tile. The rest of the treatments are carried out in the sauna, in the rest areas, or in the circular hydro-spa pool.

Opening date: 2006
Photography: © Richard Davies

Services

Sauna, hydromassage, massages, solarium, beauty salon

Web

www.virginholidays.co.uk

The steam-shower rooms, the sauna, and the circular hydro-spa pool are the essential elements of this airport spa.

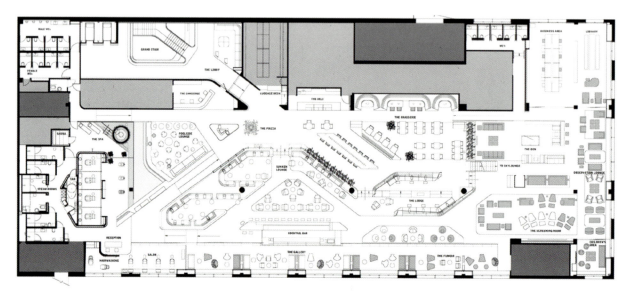

Plan

Resorts

In the search for a new spirituality or the desire for indulgence in an idyllic setting, resorts offer the best possible solution for the well-being culture.

Uma Paro

Paro, Bhutan

Set in the heart of the Himalayan Mountains, in the land of the thunder dragon, stands the Kingdom of Bhutan. In this pristine Buddhist nation, which opened its borders to the world in 1974, yoga and meditation are part of daily life, and the country serves as an ideal setting for spiritual enlightenment, relaxation, and re-energizing.

Conceived as a holistic center more than a traditional spa, Como Shambhala Retreat at Uma Paro has a yoga pavilion with views of the forest, rivers and rural villages of the Paro valley.

It features four treatment rooms, yoga studio, separate male/female steam rooms, hot stone bath house, gym and indoor pool with outdoor sundeck. Besides that, nine of the 29 villas house a private treatment room.

Thanks to cooperation with the traditional medicine hospital in the region, organic substances are basic ingredients in the therapies as well as in the cuisine. The influence of neighboring India has led to Ayurveda being introduced in many of the treatments.

Guests are encouraged to experience Bhutan through physical activities like hiking, trekking and biking, and cultural activities that complete the experience of this holistic health center.

Opening date: 2004
Photography: © Como Resorts and Hotels

Services

Yoga, steam rooms, indoor swimming pool, holistic treatments, gym

Web

www.comoshambhala.bz

Nine of the villas boast a private treatment area.

W Retreat & Spa

North Ari Atoll, Maldives

Peace, silence, beauty and simple elegance merge to create the aura this Away Spa at the W Retreat & Spa emits. Situated in the Indian Ocean opposite a coral reef, the retreat is built on a floating teak platform, its design a mix of traditional architecture and modern lines with nature at the forefront.

In contrast to traditional resort spas, the Away Spa is not housed in a building. Instead, there is an open-plan system to allow greater interaction with the sea.

Inspiration comes from the traditional dhow, or the sailboats with their elegant silhouettes. Dhows are often seen sailing along the region's coasts. With this image in mind, canvas and tents are used to separate the treatment and rest areas from the rest of the hotel.

The therapies are carried out both inside and outside. There is a daybed and an immersion shower, and there are spaces for various treatments in the open air.

The teak platform at the far end of the spa—and thus nearer the sea—hosts the yoga and outdoor painting sessions. It is also an ideal spot to enjoy the Fesdu Island's magnificent sunsets.

Opening date: 2006
Photography: © W Retreat & Spa

Services
Massages, yoga, rejuvenating and beauty treatments

Web
www.starwoodhotels.com

The inspiration for the design comes from the traditional dhow, the region's traditional sailboat with a distinctive silhouette.

Designed specifically to nurture a close connection to the ocean, many of the treatments in the Away Spa are carried out in the fresh air.

Earth Spa

Hua Hin, Thailand

What at first resembles a village in the middle of the rainforest is actually a spa, compriing nine buildings in a circle, which symbolizes the center's underlying holistic philosophy.

The buildings are surrounded by a pond making it look as though they were floating. Their oval shape aims to offset the erosion caused by copious amounts of rain during the monsoon season. The cabins are made with a kind of mud—the result of mixing rice husks, straw, and recycled materials. The inspiration came from the rural villages, where interiors stay at a pleasant temperature even during the hot summer months. The architects at DWP studio worked with local communities and a Feng Shui master to adapt the classic structure to the functions of a modern spa. The facilities include four treatment rooms, each with private outdoor Jacuzzi, two steam bath rooms, a meditation space and another for relaxation. Proximity to the water provides refreshing sea breezes, and natural light flows in through an opening in each roof.

The spa, part of the global Six Senses chain and the Evason Hideaway Hua Hin, is a prime example of the holistic approach, given its natural treatments, sustainable architecture, and close relationship with the community.

Opening date: 2005
Photography: © DWP, Evason Hideaway

Services
Steam baths, massages, revitalizing and beauty treatments

Web
www.sixsenses.com/hideaway-huahin/spa.php

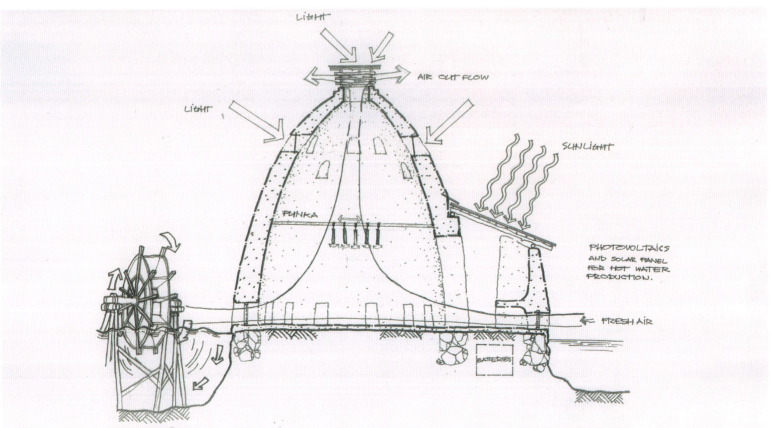

Section

The spa is a complex of nine buildings made from mud in the style of the villages in northern Thailand.

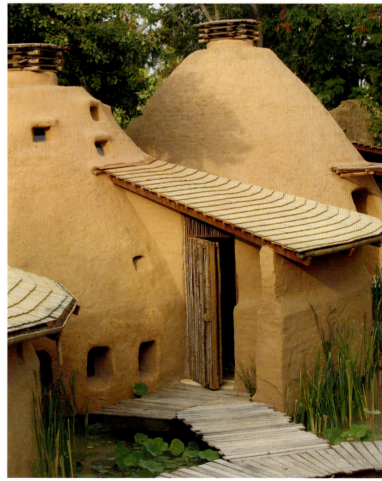

One part of the spa's programs includes discovering the benefits of meditation and how to use this in today's modern world.

Porto Elounda Deluxe Resort

Crete, Greece

Enjoying a bubble bath on a terrace with views of the Mediterranean, or immersing oneself in the thalassotherapy pool while gazing into the skies over Greek islands; this experience is only possible at the Six Senses spa in Elounda. Located in Mirabello Bay, the resort boasts 500 feet of private beach, an executive nine-hole golf course, a golf academy and sizeable terraces with pools. The traditional cretan elements in the architecture and interior design of the hotel complex assume a more modern air in the ultracool spa.

From the moment visitors enter the reception area, they are impressed with the murals, water, stone, glass, and wood, which create a fantastic setting. This is merely an introduction to the "tepidarium," where water is kind. It is transparent in the waterfall, bubbling in the glass swimming pools, and shining in the elevated glass ponds.

The thermal suites, modeled after the Finnish sauna and traditional Roman steam baths, include a series of rooms, the last one of which houses a cold plunge pool.

One of the more original therapies offered by the spa is the Ottoman hammam, with rejuvenating treatments. Another unique aspect is the Therapy Suite, a small private spa offering a sauna, a steam room, a pool with hydromassage, an outdoor bubble bath, and relaxation spaces.

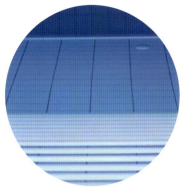

Opening date: 2006
Photography: © Dimitris Poupalos

Services

Massages, hydrotherapy, thalassotherapy, sauna, steam baths

Web

www.portoelounda.com

In the reception area, the melding of impressive murals, water, stone, glass and wood creates a fantastic setting.

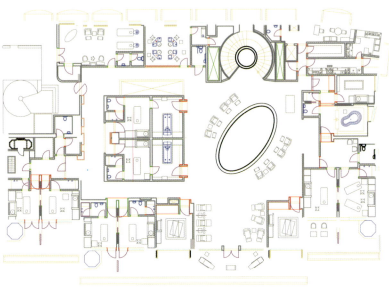

Plans

The hydromassage pool has both an interior and exterior section, so extraordinary seascapes can be enjoyed while the skin is being purified.

Zeavola

Phi Phi Island, Thailand

Inspired by the wonders and essence of rural Thailand, the spa at Zeavola boutique resort merges vibrant colors, and natural aromas with the advantages of an ancient culture devoted to rejuvenating the body and nourishing the soul and spirit. This center of well-being occupies one part of the resort, with fifty-two-villas scattered along the edge of a long white sand beach on the island of Phi Phi, only an hour from Phuket by speedboat. The 650-square-foot cabins are decorated with traditional textiles and boast private gardens where showers can be taken in the fresh air. Each villa has three hotel employees to attend to the needs of the guests.

The hotel spa has six treatment rooms for couples, three of which have a shower and rest area; two are reserved for Thai massages, and the last one has a spa with Jacuzzi, shower, and terrace.

The essence of ancient healing techniques, as well as a broad understanding of the therapies are present throughout the treatment menu, which includes, for example, sesame compresses for dry skin, exfoliation with organic coffee and spices, and body cleansing with seasalt, herbs, and mint.

The resort gardens and the beachfront also serve as therapy areas, intimately linked to nature. After all, the name of the hotel itself is taken from the exotic Scaevola Taccada tree, also known locally as Rak Talay, which means "love the sea."

Opening date: 2005
Photography: © Noppatad Leerasettakorn

Services
Steam baths, sauna, hydromassage, Thai massage, and invigorating body treatments

Web
www.zeavola.com

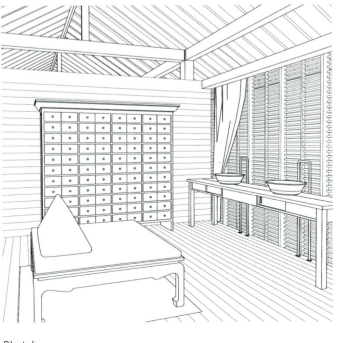

Sketch

Each one of the 52 villas of the hotel boasts a private garden, many of which also have outdoor showers.

One&Only Reethi Rah

North Male Atoll, Maldives

Located on one of the 1,190 islands that make up the garland known as the Maldives, the Reethi Rah resort's spa blends the Oriental with the local. It was designed by ESPA, the world's foremost spa consultant.

Built with stone walls and straw roofs, the traditional style of the eight villas in the spa complex is meant to maintain a harmonious nexus with nature.

Couples searching for total isolation can enjoy private floating suites which remain linked to the island by wooden walkways. Each one of these luxury cabins is equipped with daybeds, individual massage tables, baths for two, a steam room, and a deck with dining terrace.

The Chi wing, close to the suites, appears to be suspended above the ocean, creating an atmosphere of positive energy on a platform ideal for clearing the mind and balancing the body before going to a yoga or meditation session.

Hydromassage pools, ice fountains, steam baths, tropical rain or fog showers with gentle mint aromas serve as stimulating preparation to the therapies—all drawn from ancient oriental cultures and combined with new techniques of relaxation and rejuvenation.

Opening date: 2006
Photography: © Barbara Kraft

Services

Steam baths, Thai massage and shiatsu, holistic therapies, hydromassage, yoga

Web

www.oneandonlyresorts.com

Some of the spa treatments, such as the bath rituals, the exfoliations, and the Thai, shiatsu, and Bali massages originate in India and Sri Lanka.

Kempinski Hotel Barbaros Bay

Bodrum, Turkey

Located on the breathtakingly beautiful Barbaros Bay, the Kempinski Hotel enjoys spectacular views over the turquoise waters and golden sand of the Aegean Sea. Its modern design adapts to the geography of the place and employs ancient traditions of this region, which is characterized by a certain multiculturalism. The 60,000-square-foot Six Senses spa follows suit with a blend of contemporary design, traditional Turkish hospitality, and an Asian treatment philosophy.

The sixteen individual and couple therapy zones include three hammams, (Turkish baths) illuminated with natural light, an indoor pool with hydro-massage, and watsu pool (a therapy in hot water combining elements of shiatsu with yoga).

All the treatments begin with a traditional Thai foot massage followed by a cup of ginger tea. The therapies are grouped according to their nature—sensory, Asian, facial, and body. The series of programs all have specific objectives, such as reaching harmony through reiki, crystal healing, full body massage, and "candles in the ears"—a practice inspired by the Shamans and their pursuit of harmony.

The spa incorporates a gym with high-tech equipment and two outdoor pools that look as though they go on forever and merge into the Aegean Sea.

Opening date: 2006
Photography: © Jorg Sundermann

Services
Turkish baths, massages, sauna, watsu, holistic therapies, beauty treatments

Web
www.kempinski-bodrum.com

The spa is a mixture of ultramodern design, the traditional Turkish welcome and the Asian wellness philosophy.

The treatment zone includes three hammams, an indoor hydromassage pool, a watsu pool, a gym, two outdoor pools, and a private spa zone.

COMO Shambhala Estate

Ubud, Bali

Unlike resorts that offer a spa as just another service, the Estate was conceived and designed as a unique residential health retreat that combines holistic treatments with state of the art facilities.

The surroundings dominated by forests, rice fields, and mist-wrapped mountains create a beautiful and almost magical setting for the 23 acres resort. The area is renowned for its natural springs which have well-documented properties beneficial to health.

The 31 suites are grouped into five residences, five villas, three garden villas, and two retreat villas each one with a unique name and style. Guests can choose from an extensive menu of treatments or take part in one of six programs. The facilities include a hydrotherapy pool, a sauna, steam rooms, an open-air gym, a yoga area, and a studio dedicated to Pilates. The surroundings are also the perfect setting for activities, and the mountains, rivers, volcanoes, and valleys can be used for training in diverse disciplines.

The resort is host to frequent seminars and programs given by visiting masters with subject areas such as energy curing in Tibetan Buddhism or naturopathy.

Whether it is the lush setting or the constant inspiration from the activities, or both, it is nearly impossible not to change lifestyle after having visited the Estate.

Opening date: 2005
Photography: © Como Resorts and Hotels

Services
Yoga, Pilates, martial arts, outdoor circuit training, holistic therapies, sauna, hydromassage, steam bath, seminars

Web
www.comoshambhala.bz

The area is renowned for its natural thermal springs.

As well as traditional spa therapies, the Estate is a holistic healing center visited by renowned spiritual masters.

Guests can choose from an extensive menu of treatments or take part in one of six programs.

Bulgari Resort

Pecatu, Bali

Located close to the village of Pecatu and the impressive Pura Luhur Uluwatu Temple, the Bulgari Resort, at more than 500 feet above sea level, is a luxury wellness resort that offers unbeatable views of the Indian Ocean.

The complex consists of 59 villas, a swimming pool, and a courtyard with a tropical garden that represents a contemporary take on traditional Bali design.

The hotel was built and furnished with hand-cut volcanic stone, rich exotic timbers, and refined fabrics. Right at the heart of the complex, the spa rises up like an old Javan Joglo house that can be instantly dismantled. An outdoor relaxation lounge, a yoga area, and a pool comprise the core of the building. There are also rainwater showers, saunas with aromatic steam, six treatment rooms, and two royal pavilions with outdoor gardens.

One of the highlights of the wide range of European, Balinese, and Asian-inspired treatments is the Double Bulgari Royal Lulur, a ritual experience carried out by two therapists per client who work in synchronized harmony. They do a body massage rich in herbs and exotic oils, or a hot-stone therapy in which heated volcanic basalt stones are placed on energy points—chakras that will induce deep relaxation and dissolve stress.

Opening date: 2006
Photography: © Bulgari

Services

European, Balinese, and Asian-inspired holistic therapies, sauna, aromatherapy, steam baths, hydromassage, gym, and beauty salon

Web

www.bulgarihotels.com

The spa treatments and facials that are offered in the intimacy of the villas are also available on the beach and in the pool at dawn or sunset.

Directory

AHÍN WELLNESS & SPA
Architect: Caparra Entelman & Asociados
Arenales 1938, 5° A
C1123 AAD Buenos Aires, Argentina
Tel.: +54 11 4812 5119
info@caparra-entelman.com.ar
www.caparra-entelman.com.ar

AMAN-I-KHÁS
Architect: Jean-Michel Gathy/Denniston
UBN Tower, 26th Floor
10, Jalan P. Ramlee
50250 Kuala Lumpur, Malaysia
Tel.: +603 2031 3418
denniston@denniston.com.my
www.denniston.com.my

BLOWW
Architect: Claridge Architects Ltd
Unit 11, The Tay Building
2A Wrentham Avenue
London NW10 3HA, UK
Tel.: +44 20 8969 9223
info@claridgedesign.com
www.claridgedesign.com

BLUE LAGOON
Architect: VA Arkitektar
Borgatún 6
101 Reykjavík, Iceland
Tel.: +354 5306 990
vaarkitektar@vaarkitektar.is
www.vaarkitektar.is

BOTTA'S BERGOASE
Architect: Mario Botta
Via Ciani 16
CH-6904 Lugano, Switzerland
Tel.: +41 91 9728 625
info@botta.ch
www.botta.ch

BULGARI RESORT
Architect: Antonio Citterio and Partners
Via Cerva 4
20122 Milan, Italy
Tel.: +39 02 763 8801
info@antoniocitterioandpartners.it
www.antoniocitterioandpartners.it

COMO SHAMBHALA ESTATE
Architect: Cheong Yew Kuan/Area Designs
45 Cantonment Road
Singapore 089748, Singapore
Tel.: +65 67355995
area@indo.net.id

COWSHED AT CLARENDON CROSS
Design: Ilse Crawford/Studioilse
4th Floor, 41 Great Guildford Street
London SE1 OES, UK
Tel.: +44 20 7928 0550
ilse@studioilse.com
www.studioilse.com

COWSHED SPA AT THE VIRGIN ATLANTIC CLUBHOUSE
Architect: Softroom
341 Oxford Street
London W1C 2JE, UK
Tel.: +44 20 7408 0864
softroom@softroom.com
www.softroom.com

DOLCE & GABBANA BEAUTY FARM
Design: Pietro Ferruccio Laviani
Via de Amicis 53
20123 Milan, Italy
Tel.: +39 02 8942 1426
info@laviani.com
www.laviani.com
Decoration: David Chipperfield
Cobham Mews, Agar Grove
London NW1 9SB, UK
Tel.: +44 20 7267 9422
info@davidchipperfield.co.uk
www.davidchipperfield.co.uk

DUET TIANA
Architect: Alonso Balaguer y
Arquitectos Asociados
Bac de Roda 40
08019 Barcelona, Spain
Tel.: +34 933 034 160
Príncipe Vergara 118, 1°B
28002 Madrid, Spain
Tel.: +34 915 238 054
studio@alonsobalaguer.com
www.alonsobalaguer.com

EARTH SPA
Architect: DWP – Design Worldwide Partnership
The Dusit Thani Building
Level 11, 946 Rama IV Road
Bangkok 10500, Thailand
Tel.: +66 2267 3939
thailand@dwp.com
www.dwp.com

EDGE LOTUS
Architect: Hiroshi Nakamura &
NAP Architects
Sky Heights 3-1-9-5F
Tamagawa, Setagaya-ku
158-0094 Tokyo, Japan
Tel.: +81 3 3709 7936
nakamura @nakamura.info
www.nakam.info

GEOMÉTRICAS THERMAL SPA
Architect: Germán del Sol
Camino las Flores 11441
7591295 Las Condes, Santiago, Chile
contacto@germandelsol.cl
www.germandelsol.cl

GRANNY.M
Architect: Hiroyuki Miyake Design Office
106, 2-2-18 Jouganji Kita-ku
462-0021 Nagoya Aichi, Japan
Tel.: +81 52 917 5603
info@hiroyukimiyake.com
www.hiroyukimiyake.com

HARNN HERITAGE SPA
Design: Vitoon Kunalungkarn/
IAW Company Ltd
189-11 Soi Panich-anan Sukhumvit 71
Wattana, Bangkok 10110, Thailand
Tel.: +66 2713 1237
iaw334iaw.co.th
www.iaw.co.th

KEMPINSKI HOTEL BARBAROS BAY
Architect: Sinan Kafadar/
Metex Design Group
Büyükdere Caddesi, Oyan ı hani 108, 1
Kat:1, Esentepe, Istanbul, Turkey
Tel.: +90 212 2880527

MERANO THERMAL BATHS
Architect: Matteo Thun and Partners
Via Appiani 9, 1
20121 Milan, Italy
Tel.: +39 02 655 691
Fax: +39 02 657 0646
info@matteothun.com
www.matteothun.com

NOVA KÖFLACH THERMAL SPA
Architect: Team A Graz
Merangasse 35
A 8010 Graz, Austria
Tel.: +43 316 3233 32 0
office@team-a-graz.at
www.team-a-graz.at

ONE&ONLY REETHI RAH
Design: ESPA International
ESPA House
Crosby Way, Farnham
Surrey GU9 7XX, UK
Tel.: +44 12 5235 2231
info@espainternational.co.uk
www.espaonline.com

ONSEN RETREAT AND SPA
Architect: Grounds Kent Architects
1st Floor, 30 Henry Street
6160 Fremantle, Australia
Tel.: +61 8 9335 7622
gka@gkaperth.com
www.gkaperth.com

PORTO ELOUNDA DELUXE RESORT
Architect: Syntax
Brickhouse 80b High Street
Burnham, Berkshire SL1 7JT, UK
Tel.: +44 16 2866 5555
info@syntaxuk.com
www.syntaxuk.com

SÁMAS SPA
Architect: Michele Sweeney/
Oppermann Associates
Unit D1, The Millhouse, The Steelworks
Foley Street, Dublin 1, Ireland
Tel.: +353 1 8899800
architecture@oppermann.ie
www.oppermann.ie

SEA SAUNA
Architect: Scheiwiller Svensson
Arkitektkontor
Åsögatan 119
116 24 Stockholm, Sweden
Tel.: +46 8 5060 1650
info@ssark.se
www.ssark.se

SPA CAUDALIE AT THE MARQUÉS DE RISCAL HOTEL
Architect: Frank Gehry and Partners
12541 Beatrice Street
Los Angeles, CA 90066, USA
Tel.: +1 310 482 3000
info@foga.com
www.foga.com

SPACIOMM
Design: Sandra Tarruella & Isabel López
Interioristas
Putget 6, pasaje particular, local 8
08006 Barcelona, Spain
Tel./Fax: +34 932 531 169
proyectos@tarruellalopez.com
www.tarruellalopez.com

SPORTPLAZA MERCATOR
Architect: VenhoevenCS
Hoogte Kadijk 143 F15
NL1018 BH Amsterdam, Holland
Tel.: +31 20 6228 210
info@venhoevencs.nl
www.venhoevencs.nl

SPOT REMOTA
Architect: Germán del Sol
Camino las Flores 11441
7591295 Las Condes, Santiago, Chile
contacto@germandelsol.cl
www.germandelsol.cl

STUDIO W
Architect: Arthur de Mattos Casas
Rua Capivari 160, Pacaembu
01246-020 São Paulo, Brazil
Tel.: +55 11 3664 7700
casas@arthurcasas.com.br
www.arthurcasas.com.br

TEN SPA
Design: Belinda Albo Design Studio Inc.
149 Brooke Avenue
Toronto, ON M5M 2K3, Canada
Tel.: +416 3227 874
belalbo@rogers.com
www.thehomeadvisor.ca

THE PENINSULA SPA
Architect: Chhada Siembieda & Associates
Suite 2105, 21st Floor
118 Connaught Road West
Hong Kong
csal@chhadasiembieda.com.hk
www.csa-hk.com
Tel.: +852 25212191

THE RITZ CARLTON SPA
Architect: Kollin Altomare Architects
5826 E. Naples Plaza
Long Beach, CA 90803, USA
Tel.: +1 562 856 1256
infoKAA1898@kollinaltomare.com
www.kollinaltomare.com

THE STANDARD
Design: Shawn Hausman Design
1285 N. Crescent Heights Blvd., Suite L
Los Angeles, CA 90046, USA
Tel.: +1 323 656 0898
info@shawnhausmandesign.com
www.shawnhausmandesign.com
Andre Balazs Properties
The Puck Building
295 Lafayette St., 7th Floor
New York, NY 10012, USA
Tel.: +1 212 226 5656
www.andrebalazsproperties.com

THERMAE BATH SPA
Architect: Grimshaw Architects
57 Clerkenwell Road
London EC1M 5NG, UK
Tel.: +44 20 7291 4141
info@grimshaw-architects.com
www.grimshaw-architects.com

UMA PARO
Architect: Cheong Yew Kuan/Area Designs
45 Cantonment Road
Singapore 089748, Singapore
Tel.: +65 6735 5995
area@indo.net.id

W RETREAT & SPA
Architect: Ecoid
11 Stamford Road, # 04-06, Capitol Bldg.
Singapore 178884, Singapore
Tel.: +65 6337 5119
info@ecoid.com
www.ecoid.com

WINTER BATH AT SPREE RIVER
Architect: Gil Wilk/Wilk-Salinas
Architekten, Thomas Freiwald
Eichenstrasse 4
12435 Berlin, Germany
Tel.: +49 30 533 203 65
gil.wilk@gmx.de
www.gil-wilk.de
mail@thomasfreiwald.com
www.thomasfreiwald.com

WONDERLAND
Design: Michael Angelo
418 W. 13th St.
New York, NY 10014, USA
Tel.: +1 212 524 2800
mail@wonderlandbeautyparlor.com
www.wonderlandbeautyparlor.com

XEL-HA
Architect: Jun Aoki & Associates
Harajuku New Royal Bldg. #701
3-38-11 Shibuya-ku
150-0001 Tokyo, Japan
Tel.: +81 3 5414 3471
www.aokijun.com

ZEAVOLA
Architect: Amata Luphaiboon/Department
of Architecture Co. Ltd
Quanchai Panitpichetvong
12/75 Metric Bldg., 3 Soi
Premier 1 Branch 14
Srinakarin Road, Prawet, Bangkok 10250,
Thailand
Tel.: +66 2743 4512 2
Fax: +66 2743 4516
dept.of.arch@gmail.com